PAID

Finding Out About
VICTORIAN LAW AND ORDER

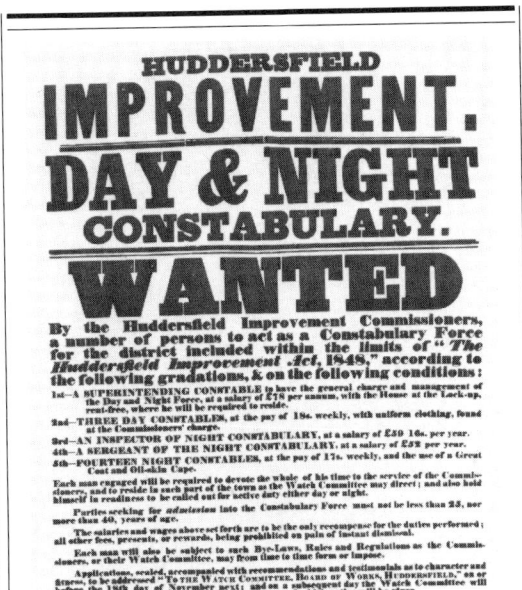

Alan Evans

B.T. Batsford Limited, London

Contents

Introduction	3
Useful Sources	4
Law and Order Statistics	6
Drink and Crime	8
Crime and the Growth of Towns	10
Street Crime	12
Burglars and House-Breaking	14
Juvenile Crime	16
Rural Crime	18
Riots and Terrorism	20
The Mid-Nineteenth-Century Police	22
Policemen's Lives	24
Courts, Judges and Sentences	26
Prisons and Hulks	28
The Separate and Silent Systems	30
Transportation to Australia	32
Dartmoor Prison	34
Capital Punishment	36
Law and Order in the West Country	38
Broadsheets and the Yellow Press	40
Victorian Detective Novels	42
Map	44
Difficult Words	45
Date List	46
Book List	47
Index	48

© Alan Evans 1988
First published 1988
Reprinted 1992

All rights reserved. No part of this publication may be reproduced, in any form or by any means, without permission from the Publisher

Typeset by Tek-Art Ltd, Kent
and printed and bound in Great Britain by
The Bath Press, Avon
for the publishers
B.T. Batsford Limited,
4 Fitzhardinge Street
London W1H 0AH

ISBN 0 7134 5659 0

Frontispiece
Recruitment poster for Huddersfield police force, 1848.

Cover illustrations
The colour illustration shows a trial in progress in a nineteenth-century court (nineteenth-century drawing hand-coloured by Frederick de Luc). The black and white photograph shows the uniform of a Victorian policeman. The illustration on the right is a "wanted" notice from February 1888.

ACKNOWLEDGMENTS

The photograph on page 11 is reproduced by kind permission of the Barnardo Photographic Archive. Photographs on pages 23, 34, 38 and 39 were taken by the Author. The map on page 44 was drawn by R.F. Brien. All remaining illustrations are from the Author's collection or from the Publishers' archives.

Introduction

When Queen Victoria was born in 1819, Britain was a very disorderly and undisciplined country. Crime, especially theft of all kinds, was common and many people feared that the nation was on the brink of revolution. Yet most Britons rejected the idea of police forces being introduced. They prided themselves on being free men and believed that an efficient police force would turn them into slaves. If there was a choice between liberty and order then Britons preferred to be free and to take their chances of being robbed or attacked.

This attitude may seem strange to us, but life was hard in the early nineteenth century and Britons were an unruly and independent people. They loved brutal sports like bullock-baiting, bare-knuckle boxing matches, and quarter-staff and cudgel playing. They fought pitched battles in the streets at election times, treated women and children working in the growing number of cotton mills harshly, and flogged soldiers and sailors for minor offences. It is not, therefore, surprising that laws were severe and prison conditions dreadful.

By the end of Victoria's reign much had changed. In 1837 there was only one proper police force in Britain – the Metropolitan Police Force in London. Over the next thirty years every county and sizeable town established a similar force. Changes in the police were paralleled by changes in the punishment system. There was a growing feeling that it was wrong to execute people for minor crimes like shoplifting. This led in the 1820s and 1830s to the abolition of the death sentence for this offence and for preposterous crimes such as being disguised within the Royal Mint, injuring Westminster Bridge and even impersonating out-pensioners of Greenwich Hospital. This in turn, together with the growing reluctance of the Australian colonies to accept any more

Prisoners at work on the treadwheel in the late nineteenth century. Used as part of the "hard-labour" system, the treadwheel was invented in 1818 by an engineer, William Cubitt, and it was used in prisons until 1898.

convicts from Britain, resulted in the development of the modern prison system. Between 1837 and 1901 there were some 15 million receptions into prisons in England and Wales. Wicked neglect was gradually replaced by benign tyranny as reformers tried to perfect methods of both punishing and reforming prisoners.

By 1901 a system of law and order, similar in many ways to today's, was in place. Britain was a much more orderly and less crime-ridden society than it had been 100 years before. These changes were due in part to the new police forces and prisons, but the spread of compulsory education in the later nineteenth century, which helped remove children from the streets, and a gradual improvement in the standard of living also helped reduce crime and disorder.

Today, television, radio, newspapers and magazines bombard us with facts and opinions about crime and the police. In 1984 there were 3.5 million recorded crimes, including 1.8 million cases of theft, nearly 900,000 burglaries and over 100,000 violent crimes. We have 135,000 policemen and a prison population of 50,000. In 1984, two million offenders were sentenced by the courts. In 1884, when the population was about half what it is today, there were only 39,000 policemen and if there were 28,000 people in prison a mere 14,500 people were tried in England and Wales, of whom 11,000 were convicted. This comparison between late Victorian and late twentieth-century Britain may suggest that crime has grown in the last hundred years, but it must be remembered that society has changed – many of the two million offenders sentenced by the courts in 1984 were charged with motoring offences. Like people in the early nineteenth century we too are faced with a law and order crisis. It seems certain that in the next few years our police and penal systems will be as radically reformed as they were during the reign of Queen Victoria between 1837 and 1901.

Useful Sources

Part of the fun of being a junior historian is carrying out your own investigations into the past. There are several ways in which you can discover more about law and order in Victorian times in your own area.

1. PEOPLE TO ASK
Your nearest large library and local museum will have all sorts of useful material. The librarians will be able to give you advice on what information they hold, especially if you are clear about what you are interested in.

2. BUILDINGS
There are probably Victorian police stations in your area. You may also find that not far from where you live there is a Victorian prison. It ought to have the initials V.R. carved above the main door. You can look at the outside of prisons, studying the style of architecture and estimating the height of the walls but do not act in a suspicious manner or ignore notices which forbid the photographing of prisoners or prison staff. If you are visiting Cornwall or are lucky enough to live there the prison at Bodmin is open to the public.

3. MUSEUMS
Many museums of local history contain exhibits which will help you understand aspects of Victorian law and order. The Ypres Tower Museum in Rye (Sussex), Anne of Cleves' House Museum in Lewes (Sussex), the Guildhall Museum in Rochester, and the Castle Museum in York all contain interesting exhibits (policemen's truncheons and rattles for instance). A full list of museums is contained in a magazine published each year called *Museums and Galleries in Great Britain and Ireland.* Your local reference library will have a copy.

4. VISUAL MATERIAL
a) Local libraries and museums may well have old photographs of your area, which may

include pictures of policemen, police stations and prisons of the Victorian period.

b) Today there are a growing number of books of Victorian photographs. Two useful ones are *Victorian and Edwardian Police and Prisons* by J. Whitmore (Batsford 1978) and *A Hundred Years Ago: Britain in the 1880s in Words and Pictures* by C. Ford and B. Harrison (Penguin 1983).

c) Your nearest main library will probably hold copies of Victorian magazines like the *Illustrated London News* and *Graphic* which had many illustrated articles on law and order. *Punch* often had cartoons poking fun at the police.

5. WRITTEN SOURCES (See Book List, page 47)

There is one source which we cannot use. Victorian criminals left little behind in their own words. Usually what we have is the criminal world seen through the eyes of J.P.s, policemen, novelists and prison chaplains. You must try to bridge this difficult gap by using your historical imagination.

If you want to find out more about today's problems you could build up a scrapbook of newspaper articles. Papers like the *Guardian*, *The Times*, the *Independent* and the *Daily Telegraph* often have informative articles on law and order.

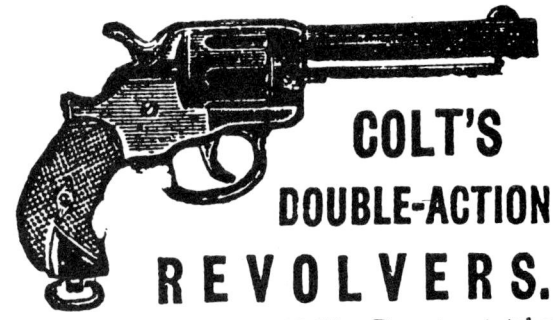

COLT'S DOUBLE-ACTION REVOLVERS.

·450 cal., as supplied to H. M. War Department, takes the Boxer Service Cartridge; ·380 cal., for Travellers and House Protection.
COLT'S DERINGER, for the Vest Pocket.
COLT'S NEW B.L. *SHOT GUNS* now ready.
Price List free. Address,
COLT'S FIREARMS CO., 14, Pall Mall, London.

This advertisement is taken from Punch's Almanack, *1882. The company makes the same products today although it is no longer so easy to buy a revolver as it was in Queen Victoria's reign.*

Convicts leaving Princeton Gaol to go to work on Dartmoor in the late nineteenth century.

Law and Order Statistics

The nineteenth century was a great age for facts. "What I want", says Mr Gradgrind in Charles Dickens's *Hard Times* "is Facts . . . Facts alone are wanted in life." Throughout the period covered by this book, statistics on crime, police and prisons can be found in government and parliamentary publications, in books and magazines. These "facts" are often difficult to use, however. Even today many crimes occur which are not reported to the police and criminologists think that nearly twice as many burglaries are committed than are recorded by the police.

"LIES, DAMNED LIES AND STATISTICS"

Statistics about crime are very difficult to handle. This is as true today as it was in Victoria's reign. The introduction to *Judicial Statistics, 1856-1873*, published in 1874, pointed out that:

> The commitments for trial in . . . 1856 show an unprecedented decrease. . . . This must . . . be largely attributed to the extended powers of Justices of the Peace [i.e. magistrates] to deal summarily [i.e. in a trial without a jury] in cases of larceny [theft] under the Criminal Justice Act of 1855.

The *Quarterly Review* in 1874 pointed out another factor which is important in interpreting criminal statistics:

> . . . our readers in comparing the numbers of criminals in more recent years with those of an earlier period must . . . remember the great additions which have been made to the population of the country. The number of criminals is not much more than half in 1873, out of 23 millions of people, of what it was in 1841, out of 16 millions. . . . In other words, whilst the growth of population has been nearly 45 per cent, crime has actually diminished by about 25 per cent.

What two factors should we therefore bear in mind when trying to interpret criminal statistics?

A RISE IN CRIME?

Frederick Engels (1820-95) wrote his famous book *The Condition of the Working Class in England* in 1844-5. Engels was later to be the friend and political partner of Karl Marx, the founder of communism.

> . . . with the extension of the proletariat [industrial working class], crime has increased in England, and the British have become the most criminal in the world. . . . The numbers of arrests for criminal offences reached in the years: 1805, 4,065; 1815, 7,898; 1825, 14,437; 1835. 20,731; 1842. 31,309 in England and Wales. . . . Of these arrests, in 1842, 4,497 were made in Lancashire alone . . . and 4,094, in Middlesex including London . . . so that two districts which include great cities with large proletarian populations produced one-fourth of the total amount of crime, though their population is far from forming one-fourth of the whole.

Calculate the percentage of crime in 1842 that was committed in Lancashire and Middlesex. Can you deduce from this extract how Engels explained the seven-fold increase in crime in 37 years? (If you look at pages 10-11 you will get some clues.)

A FALL IN CRIME?

The following figures, showing the number of commitments (i.e. the number of persons held in prison awaiting trial), are taken from the *Quarterly Review*, a conservative magazine, for October 1874.

Using the figures supplied by Engels and the *Quarterly Review* draw a graph showing the number of commitments between 1805 and 1873.

1842..31,309	1853..27,057	1864..19,506
1843..29,591	1854..29,539	1865..19,614
1844..26,542	1855..25,972	1866..18,849
1845..24,303	1856..19,437	1867..18,971
1846..25,107	1857..20,269	1868..20,091
1847..28,833	1858..17,855	1869..19,318
1848..30,349	1859..16,674	1870..17,578
1849..27,816	1860..15,999	1871..16,269
1850..26,813	1861..18,326	1872..14,801
1851..27,960	1862..20,001	1873..14,893
1852..27,510	1863..20,818	

METROPOLITAN POLICE.

RETURN of the Number of MEN of each Rank and Class of the METROPOLITAN POLICE serving on the First Day of January 1840; also the RATE OF PAY of each Class, and the ALLOWANCES.

NUMBER.	RANK.	CLASS	AMOUNT PER ANNUM.
			£. s. d.
1	Inspecting Superintendent	-	400 - -
1	Superintendent	-	300 - -
16	- ditto	-	250 - -
73	Inspectors	-	118 6 -
349	Sergeants	-	63 14 -
250	Constables	1st	54 12 -
2,527	- ditto	2d	49 8 -
269	- ditto	3d	44 4 -
	The sergeants and constables are allowed clothing, and each married man of these two ranks is allowed 40 pounds weight of coals weekly throughout the year; each single man is allowed 40 pounds weight weekly during six winter months, and 20 pounds weight weekly for the remainder of the year.	Allowances.	
3	Inspectors	-	127 15 -
1	- ditto	-	118 6 -
1	- ditto	-	100 - -
1	- ditto	-	91 - -
16	Constables	1st	81 18 -
11	- ditto	2d	72 16 -
38	- ditto	3d	63 14 -
1	Principal Inspector	-	140 - -
1	Inspector	1	100 - -
6	- ditto	2d	90 - -
6	- ditto	3d	80 - -
8	- ditto	4th	75 - -
30	Constables	1st	59 16 -
40	- ditto	2d	54 12 -
		£.	2,535 1 -

C. Rowan.

IDENTIFYING PRISONERS

In 1887 the Chaplain of Clerkenwell Gaol in London, the Reverend J.W. Horsley, wrote in his book *Jottings from Jail* that:

> We take very little notice of names and ages in prison, as from various reasons they are apt to alter with each entrance. Thus Frederick Lane, aged 15, has just been sentenced to 18 months imprisonment. He has previously been in custody as Alfred Miller, aged 15, John Smith, aged 16, John Collins, aged 16, John Kate, aged 17, John Klythe, aged 17, and John Keytes, aged 17.

Why would a prisoner want to be thought of as a first-time offender? What would make the problem of identifying prisoners easier?

◀ What was the total strength of the Metropolitan Police in 1840? Can you calculate the wage bill of the force?

Drink and Crime

Alcohol was seen by many Victorian commentators as a prime cause of crime. William Hoyle wrote angrily in 1876 that beer and spirits filled "the land with drunkenness, crime... [and] insanity...".

"SHADOW'S" GLASGOW

A writer calling himself "Shadow" made a study of Glasgow in 1858. One policeman he questioned estimated that there were 500 or 600 drunks every evening on Argyle Street, one of the city's main roads. On Saturday, in particular, the people flocked to the pubs:

> One can scarcely realise the enormous number of these houses, with their flaring gas lights in frosted globes, and brightly gilded spirit casks... with the occasional mirror at the extreme end of the shop reflecting at once in fine perspective the waters of a granite fountain fronting the door, and the entrance of poor broken down victims, who stand in pitiful burlesque in their dirty rags, amid all this pomp and mocking grandeur.

Nearly 9000 people every year in Glasgow were charged with being drunk and disorderly. Many of these could only be got to the police station in wheelbarrows!

This picture is from Max Schlesinger's book Saunterings In and Around London *(1853). It shows the interior of a "gin palace". Note the children and babies. Do you think children should be allowed in public houses?*

DRINK-CAUSED CRIME

In his book *Prisons and Prisoners* (1898) the Reverend J.W. Horsley (1845-1921), the Chaplain at Clerkenwell Prison in London, discussed the extent to which drink caused crime:

> ...half the cases of common assault, three-quarter of assaults on the police and half the aggravated assaults were committed by drunken persons.... Cruelty to animals... and children... of these, half might fairly be considered drink caused, as also might be half of the cases of malicious damage

A DECLINE IN DRUNKENNESS

Despite Horsley's gloomy findings, social investigators like Charles Booth in his survey of London completed in 1902 found that drunkenness was declining. The annual report of the Liverpool Head Constable for 1898 also indicated this. During the year there were:

> 766 fewer cases of ... drunk and riotous [behaviour] etc. ... Licensing Acts – the number of licenced-houses in the city had been decreased by 18 public-houses and 2 beer-houses, and increased by 5 off-licences ... the number of licenced premises ... is: Public-houses: 1,865; Beer-houses: 244; Off-licenses: 153; Total 2,262. ... Drunkenness – The number of arrests during the year was 4,292, the arrests for each day of the week being as follows:– Sunday: 294; Monday: 703; Tuesday: 544; Wednesday: 452; Thursday: 401; Friday: 501; Saturday: 1,398...

Can you think why the number of cases of drunkenness was falling nationally by the end of Victoria's reign?

> **Begging** – A woman, aged 44, seven out of ten children alive, her husband fairly well to do, begged simply to get money for drink.

Horsley's argument was that in addition to nearly 170,000 cases each year in the 1890s of people being charged with being drunk and disorderly there were also a huge number of crimes committed by people under the influence of drink. Do you think the picture is similar today?

Crime and the Growth of Towns

By 1851, half of Britain's population lived in towns. By 1901, this proportion had risen to three-quarters. The rapid growth of urban Britain was a major cause of crime.

WITHOUT "NATURAL POLICE"

M.D. Hill (1792-1872), brother of Rowland Hill, the postal reformer, was a Birmingham judge for nearly 30 years. In 1852 he was examined by a House of Commons Committee on Juvenile Crime and reported:

> A century and a half ago ... there was scarcely a large town in the island ... [by a] large town I mean [one] where an inhabitant of the humbler classes is unknown to the majority of inhabitants ... by a small town, I mean a town where ... every inhabitant is more or less known to the mass of the people of the town.... in small towns there must be a sort of natural police ... operating upon the conduct of each individual, who lives, as it were, under the public eye; but in a large town, he lives ... in absolute obscurity ... which to a certain extent gives impunity [exemption from punishment].

Why does Mr Hill believe that people in large towns can escape punishment? The same argument is used today about estates where people live in tower blocks. Why might migrants to the Victorian towns have welcomed their new anonymity, and what sort of things might they have found exciting about town life? *Finding Out About Victorian Towns* will help you here.

"THE BITTER CRY"

Andrew Mearns (1837-1925) was the chief author of an influential pamphlet called *The Bitter Cry of Outcast London: An Inquiry into the Condition of the Abject Poor* (1883). This suggested:

> Few who will read these pages have any conception of what these pestilential human rookeries [the worst housing districts] are, where tens of thousands are crowded together amidst horrors which call to mind what we have learned ... of the slave ship.... One of the saddest results of this over-crowding is the inevitable association of honest people with criminals.... Who can wonder that every evil flourishes in such hotbeds of vice and disease?

The areas which have the highest crime rates today are still those which have the worst housing and poorest inhabitants.

POVERTY AND CRIME

Most Victorian analysts did not believe that crime was caused simply by poverty. In his *Report of the Royal Commission on a Constabulary Force* (1839) the famous social reformer Edwin Chadwick wrote:

> We have investigated the origin of the great mass of crime committed for the sake of property, and we find the whole ascribable to one common cause, namely, the temptations of the profit of a career of depredation [theft], as compared with the profits of honest and even well paid industry.... The

BREAD RIOTS 1861

There does seem to be evidence that more people stole in hard times than in good. The winter of 1860 saw freezing temperatures for a month. As a consequence of this, the London *Morning Star*, 18 January, 1861, reported that:

> **Owing to the continuance of the frost, and all outdoor labour being stopped, the distress and suffering that prevail ... among ... the labouring classes ... are truly horrible. ... On Tuesday night ... an attack [was] made on a large number of bakers' shops. ... on Wednesday night ... an attack was made upon many of the bakers' shops and eating-houses. ... A great many thieves ... mingled with the mob, and many serious acts of violence were committed. The mounted police ... were present, but it was impossible for them to act against so many people.**

What sort of trades and occupations would have been at risk in freezing weather in a city like London at this time?

> **notion that any considerable proportion of the crimes against property are caused by blameless poverty ... we find disproved at every step.**

What did Chadwick see as the "one common cause" of crime? Some modern historians disagree with Chadwick's findings. Certainly many children who were orphans or runaways, or who were deserted by their parents, had no alternative to theft if they were not to starve. The section of this book on "Juvenile Crime" will look in more detail at this.

This photograph shows a group of boys waiting to enter an orphanage. What signs of poverty can you detect?

EDUCATION AND RELIGIOUS INSTRUCTION

Many Victorians felt that a lack of education, especially religious education, explained the growth of crime in urban areas. In 1842 the Reverend John Sinclair published a collection of letters on this theme. One letter writer noted that:

> **There are in the manufacturing districts very large masses of people who ... have not grown up ... under the hand of early instruction ... unhappily receiving, neither in schools nor places of worship, that religious and moral instruction which is necessary to knit together the inhabitants and classes of a great country.**

Ask your R.E. teacher at school what particular teaching of the Christian church would encourage the poor to accept their lot in life and obey the laws of the land. Religious education was an integral part of elementary education from the time of the very first schools. Until the 1870s nearly all schools were run by the Church, and some still are today.

11

Street Crime

Respectable Victorians were certain that there was a separate criminal class, different from the "honest poor". This "rough working class" engaged in many sorts of crime, much of it robbery from shops or from people in the street.

This is a photograph of Thomas Parsons who was sentenced at Derby to one month's imprisonment for pocket-picking in 1865.

SHOPLIFTING

Thefts from shops took place in the nineteenth century just as they do today. The Royal Commission on a Constabulary Force (1839) gathered information from prisoners. Ellen Reece was in Salford Gaol in 1837 when she described how she had carried out her crimes:

> **Generally went two together ... [the] method was to go into a ... draper's shop ... and ask to see linen at such a price ... then ask for stockings, gloves, handkerchiefs, and when a good many things on the counter, so that they did not known the count of them, when the back was turned to reach something else, to slip them under their shawl.... Paid for the small articles and walked out gently ... and made away as fast as they could to ... "a fence".**

Look at the end of this book to find out the meaning of the word "fence". The Victorian underworld had a language all of its own: for example, "crusher" meant "policeman", "ruffles" meant "handcuffs" and "topped" meant "hanged".

"FORWARD LITTLE JHONNIES"

The *Quarterly Review* of July 1856 described how pickpockets operated.

> **Inferior classes of thieves work in small "schools" ... of a couple of women and a boy, whose little hand is capitally adapted for the work. Whilst one woman pushes, the lad attempts the pocket of the person nearest him, and the third "watches if off".... if she observes that the youth's attentions**

This illustration is from Henry Mayhew's London Labour and the London Poor. *What does the word "Mart" mean?*

ORANGE MART, DUKE'S PLACE — AN OBVIOUS TEMPTATION TO THIEVES

GARROTTING

In the early 1860s there was an epidemic in London of "garrotting". *The Annual Register* of 1862 describes how the crimes were committed:

> [It is] a method of highway plunder, which consists in one ruffian seizing an unsuspecting traveller by the neck and crushing in his throat, while another simultaneously rifles his pockets: the scoundrels then decamp [run off], leaving their victim on the ground, writhing in agony, with tongue protruding and eyes staring from their sockets, unable to give alarm or to attempt pursuit.

The article goes on to describe a garrotte attack on an M.P., and the novelist Anthony Trollope describes a similar incident in his novel *Phineas Finn* (1869). This type of robbery was ended by deterrent sentences in 1862-3. What would we call this type of robbery today?

STEALING FROM STREET STALLS

Henry Mayhew, in his classic four-volume work *London Labour and the London Poor* (1851), dealt at length with the criminal underworld. What Mayhew called "sneak thieves" ("characterized by low cunning and stealth") were active in the streets.

> In wandering along Whitechapel we see ranges of stalls on both sides of the street.... There are stalls for fruit, vegetables and oysters... [for] combs, brushes, chimney ornaments, children's toys.... the young ragged thieves... generally go in a party of three or four... watching their opportunity, they make a sudden snatch at the apples or pears... then run off, with the cry of "stop thief" ringing in their ears.... When overtaken by a police-officer... sometimes the urchin will lie down in the street and cry "let me go!" and the bystanders will take his part!

Can you explain why some people in the street might sympathize with these young thieves?

> have been noticed, she immediately draws him back with a "He Jhonny, why do you push the lady so!" Look to your pockets, good reader, when you see forward little Jhonnies about – especially at railway stations.... We [also] hear that theatres and churches, just as the people are coming out are favourite haunts...

Pickpockets still exist today, and public places like museums and airports often carry warning notices.

13

Burglars and House-Breaking

Breaking into premises, private or commercial, for the purpose of theft, was as common in the nineteenth century as it is today.

BURGLARS' TOOLS

In the appendix to Chadwick's *Report of the Royal Commission on a Constabulary Force*, a prison governor, G.C. Chesterton, described the tools used by house-breakers:

> The crow-bar is [used] to wrench open doors [with] the centre-bit ... holes are bored along the edge ... of a door ... a pocket-knife is then run along from hole to hole, the panel is removed, and the entrance is effected...
>
> The saw is used ... where the lock ... is so strong as not to be strained by the force of the crow-bar ... the piece of the door upon which the lock is fixed is cut entirely away.
>
> Pistols are now and then taken to burglaries, where the risk is great [and] where the expected booty is considerable....
>
> Nux vomica ... and prussic acid [two types of poison] are ... used to destroy animals of the canine species, which might disturb them by giving mouth.

Try putting the last paragraph into your own words – you might be able to make it a bit shorter! If your nearest large public library has a reference section, see if it contains any local newspapers dating back to Victorian times and try to find accounts of burglaries in your own area.

Housebreaking tools. Try to match these implements to those in Chesterton's description. ▶

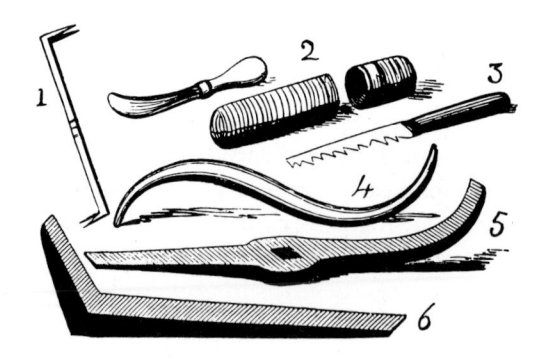

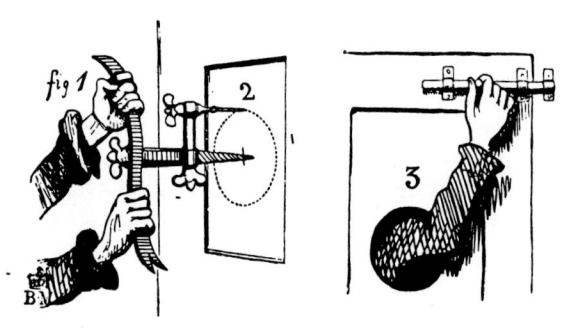

14

CRACKSMEN

Burglars, Mayhew explained, came in all classes. There were "low burglars" who specialized in robbing buildings in the poorer parts of London. Then there were the "cracksmen": they carried out burglaries

> at fashionable residences [in] the metropolis, and at the mansions of the gentry and nobility.... The houses to be robbed are carefully watched for several weeks.... The thieves ... glean information secretly as to the inmates of the house; where they sleep, and where valuable property is kept....

HOXTON'S THIEVES

Charles Booth described Hoxton at the end of the nineteenth century as "the leading criminal quarter of London", but he pointed out that:

> The number of first-class burglars is said to be very small; with most, daring takes the place of skill.... The relations of these men with the police are curious, regulated by certain rules of the game ... violence is a breach of these rules.... These men are generally known to the police, and so are the receivers into whose hands they play. Gold or silver stolen ... is promptly consigned to the melting pot. Jewellery is broken up; watches are "rechristened". The "fences" or receivers of stolen goods are of all grades, and serve every sort of thief...

Why would the police and criminals have "rules of the game"? Can you explain why stolen goods were melted, or broken up and how watches were "rechristened"?

> Burglars ... frequently do not enter the house until one or two in the morning ... they ... enter the house ... by the door or windows.
>
> On entering the house, they go about the work very cautiously and quietly, taking off their shoes.... Their chief object is to get plate, jewellery, cash and other valuables.... They often find valuables in the drawing room...

Who in these sorts of houses might, wittingly or unwittingly, help the thieves? The drawing room was the room where visitors were received. Why would this room contain "valuables"?

DEFENCES AGAINST BURGLARS

The *Quarterly Review* in June 1856 gave its readers some advice:

> Some [burglars] have become so expert that no system of bolts or bars is capable of keeping them out ... however ... a sheet of iron, on the inside of a panel [door], will often foil the most expert burglars; and all operators of this class who have opened their minds upon the subject to prison authorities admit that it is totally impossible, without alarming the inmates, to force a window that is lightly barred ... and supplied with a bell. A shutter thus protected ... will not allow the centre-bit to work without creating a motion which is sure to ring the alarum.

What sort of methods do people use today to foil burglars? Why are barred windows potentially dangerous to those who live in the house?

Juvenile Crime

A CHILD PICKPOCKET

In this extract Henry Mayhew records the statement of a man, aged 43, who had begun his criminal career as a child pickpocket:

> I ran away from home . . . when I was between 12 and 13. . . . There was nine boys of us among the lot that I joined. I worked in Fleet Street [in London] and I could make £3 a week at handkerchiefs alone, sometimes falling across a pocketbook [wallet]. The best handkerchiefs then brought 4 shillings in Field Lane. . . . I carried on in this way for about 15 months, when I was grabbed for an attempt on a gentleman's pocket by St Paul's Cathedral. . . . I had two months in the Old Horse [Bridewell Prison].

This boy's experiences were very like those of Charles Dickens' character Oliver Twist, except that there was no kindly man to rescue him from a life of crime.

Two young prisoners with a warder in the late nineteenth century. How old do you think these boys are and do you think they would be sent to prison today?

A large number of those who fell foul of the law in Victorian Britain were young people. One reason for this was that a very large proportion of the total population was under the age of 20, due to a rapid increase in the birth rate at this time.

GEORGE HEWIN ESCAPES THE BIRCH

In *The Dillen: Memories of a Man of Stratford-Upon-Avon*, George Hewin (1879-1977) recalls being involved in a schoolboy escapade which ended with a policeman being tipped into the river.

> . . . I was booked for the birch, and naturally I was took bad at the thought of it.
> Doctor Lupton . . . comes to see Cal [George's Great Aunt Caroline].
> "Where's the lad, Cal?"
> "'E's bad in bed."
> "'E weren't bad t'other night when 'e nearly got that fella drowned."
> "D'you think 'e's fit to 'ave the birch?"
> "The birch rod?" says Doctor Lupton. She put two sovereigns in his hand and he passed her a note to take to the police.
> He told me afterwards: "Behave yourself, lad, cos I can't get you off again. . . .
> Money won that. But my five pals went to Weston Reformatory for five years.

A sovereign was a gold coin worth £1.

NORWICH CASTLE GAOL

Caught poaching at the age of 12, the author of this extract was sentenced to a month's hard labour by the magistrates at Grimstone in Norfolk:

> I was taken to Norwich by train, handcuffed to a Police man. Wen I got to Norwich I was led along through the streets the same way like a real dangerous fellow. There were no Cabs then for prisners, and evry one could have a good stare at me as I went by. No doubt some people said "He have done something bad" and some may have said, "Poor kid"... but at last we arived at the Castle Entrance. A door swong open and a Turnkey [gaoler] led us inside. I shall never forget what I felt when I first saw that gloomy Place, and I was just fit to cry, but held back my tears some how. (*I Walked by Night*, by "The King of the Norfolk Poachers", 1935)

Do you think the author, who wrote this anonymously when he was an old man, was an educated person?

This girl was sentenced to seven days' imprisonment. Can you decipher her name and can you imagine what might have driven her to commit the offence?

CITY ARABS

M.D. Hill, a Birmingham judge, explained to a House of Commons Committee on Criminal and Destitute Juveniles in 1852 which children were most likely to become criminals:

> ... The first class is the children of criminals ... they are trained to crime.... Then illegitimate children.... Orphans, for obvious reasons, form another class. Foundlings [abandoned children] and step-children form a large class ... and no doubt the children of the very poor form a class.... They have all the vices and some of the virtues of savages.... they are called "City Arabs".... [The "City Arab"] is averse from settled ... employment, averse from restraint of any kind; on the other hand, he is patient of hunger, and thirst, and cold; and as to dirt, he rather takes delight in it.... he would much rather roam about at large ... than he would be at school or work...

Try to explain why each of Hill's "classes" of children were likely to be involved in crime. Do we still have a problem with street "Arabs" today?

17

Rural Crime

As late as 1871, nearly 40 per cent of England's population lived and worked in the countryside. Compared with the towns, however, there was little crime in rural areas.

GREAT MASSINGHAM, NORFOLK

In his *Refutation of the Constabulary Force Report*, written in 1839, C.D. Brereton gave an account of the crimes committed in a particular village:

> 1837.–No case of consequence.
>
> *Larceny.–Linen stealing.*
> 1838.–G. H—. On information of the robbery, the constable suspected the party, went to his house, and on searching found a part of the linen. The prisoner was apprehended by the [parish] constable and committed, and convicted, 6 months and hard labour.
>
> *Egg stealing.*
> 1838.–S. C— and W. W—, the latter only convicted, the constable having assisted in obtaining the information.
> 1839.–W. C.—. This was a case in an adjoining village. This constable was called in to examine into some trifling malicious acts, and found out in his search by night, stolen corn, of stealing which the prisoner was convicted and sentenced.
>
> *Donkey stealing.*
> 1839.–W. W— a migratory thief, birth and parentage not known. The donkey was stolen in a neighbouring town. The constable found him offering it for sale at an insufficient price...

Why do you think that the donkey thief offered the animal for sale at "an insufficient price"?

"A MURDEROUS AFFRAY"

On 7 October 1871 the Reverend Francis Kilvert noted in his diary that:

> There was a murderous affray with poachers at the Moor last night. Two keepers beaten fearfully about the head with bludgeons and one poacher, Cartwright, a Hay sawyer [who made a living by sawing timber], stabbed and his life despaired of.

Kilvert's diary is an important source of information about life in the Victorian countryside. In 1871 Kilvert was a curate in the parish of Clyro in Radnorshire, east Wales.

How did Victorian landowners try to protect their land from the attentions of poachers? If you live in a country area see if your local paper carries news of poaching – it still happens today!

A DRUNKEN POACHER

James Hawker (1836-1920), a lifelong poacher, described in his memoirs (published as *A Victorian Poacher* in 1961) how he had a lucky escape:

> Towards the end of ... 1857 ... we thought there might be a few pheasants at roost. So I put my gun in my pocket ... when I caught up with [Tom] he was leaning over a gate....
> "If I'd known you was in drink, I wouldn't have come", I said.
> "Jimmy, don't tinker," he said. "I'll be alright before we get there."
> To reach the wood we had to cross the park in front of Bradley House. When we got well inside the park gates out

Two children caught stealing by a Scottish policeman in the late nineteenth century. The photograph is very posed – can you suggest why?

"NO SCHOOL OF CRIME"

Richard Jefferies (1848-87), a Victorian writer on the countryside and rural matters, pointed out in his book *Hodge and his Masters* (1880) that:

> There is no school of crime in the country. Children are not taught [or] brought up from earliest age to beg and steal.... Though farmhouses are often situated in the most lonely places a case of burglary rarely occurs, and if it does, is still more rarely traced to a local resident.... Serious crime is comparatively scarce...

Can you come up with any explanations for the relative lack of crime in country areas?

> flew the keepers.
> Like me, Tom was a good runner... but this time drink began to tell its tale.... He rolled over like a ship in a storm... and the head keeper was soon on top of him.

Why do you think Hawker took a sawn-off rifle out poaching with him? Apart from pheasants, what else would poachers have gone after?

THE HEAVY HAND OF THE LAW

The activities of poachers like Hawker led to the Poaching Prevention Act of 1862. Joseph Arch, the organizer of a trades union for agricultural workers and later a MP explained in his autobiography (*From Ploughtail to Parliament*, 1898) how this Act affected country people:

> The day that the... Act became law was a black day for the Labourer; from that time onwards he might at any hour be subjected to the indignity of being... searched by the police officer.

The object of the Act was to prevent poaching but it was often used for a different purpose. Arch gives an example:

> It has been the custom in our neighbourhood... that if a woman was cleaning turnips in a field she might take two or three, once or twice a week.... After the Act came into operation the police set upon these women – respectable, honest, married women – searched them, brought them before the magistrates... and charged them with stealing turnips... the women were fined. It was a very great shame, and the village people were very bitter... about it.

Is there any comparison between this story and the photograph on this page?

19

Riots and Terrorism

Today, violent demonstrations, riots and terrorist attacks are frequently in the news. Victorian Britain faced strikingly similar problems.

CHARTISTS AND SOLDIERS

The Chartists felt that all men (not just the middle and upper classes) should have the right to vote in elections. Major-General Sir Charles Napier was in command of the northern district during the first outbreak of violent "Chartism" in 1839-40. This extract is from a letter written in January 1840:

> At Nottingham... the Chartists have prepared a quantity of combustibles [explosives] and are exceedingly ferocious. There are quite enough rascals among them to fire the town... but the cowardice shown is absolutely ridiculous. One night, when out with twelve dragoons [cavalrymen], a mob of 200 followed and assailed us with abuse so violent as to make me fear they would end with stones.... I rode back alone... to speak to the mob. To my surprise all fled, pushing each other down in their haste. (Sir W. Napier, *Life of General Sir Charles James Napier*, 1857)

Can you explain why the people ran away? If you want to find out more about "Chartism" you will find two useful short books listed in the bibliography. What words and phrases in this extract suggest that Napier's account is biased (one-sided)?

A TERRORIST ATTACK IN MANCHESTER

In August 1867 two "Fenians" (men who belonged to an I.R.A.-type secret society) were arrested in Manchester. On their way to prison:

> ... a young man ran out in front of [the police van]... and presenting a revolver at the driver summoned him to stop. A large body of men made their appearance... the small body of unarmed constables made a brave defence of the door.... Two... were wounded... [Sergeant] Brett... fell mortally wounded, the bullet having passed straight through the skull... the two prisoners were released.
> (*Cassells' Illustrated History of England*, 1870)

Three men were later executed for the murder of the policeman. Do you believe that violence can be justified if it is in pursuit of political aims?

This picture is from the *Graphic* and shows the ▶ London riots of 1886. St James's Palace is in the background.

20

DISTURBANCES IN BELFAST

Tension between Catholics and Protestants was as much a feature of life in Northern Ireland in the nineteenth century as it is today. The *Spectator*, a conservative weekly magazine, carried the following report on 21 August 1886:

> **Last Saturday night, Belfast was the scene of a moonlight rifle-duel between the Orangemen and the Roman Catholics, which resulted in two or three deaths, and several injuries. It is said that the duel went on for several hours without any interference of the police or soldiers ... the people of Belfast are very naturally disgusted with the incompetence shown [by the police] ... and ... are asking to have Belfast supplied with a police force on the Metropolitan type – i.e. the type of London or Dublin...**

"Orangemen" took their name from William of Orange (King William III) who led the Protestants to victory over King James II and the Roman Catholics at the Battle of the Boyne in 1690. They believed that Ireland should be ruled only by Protestants.

Reading this extract you can understand why the Royal Irish Constabulary was an *armed* police force.

This illustration is from Cassell's Illustrated History of England *(c. 1871). It shows a Belfast riot in 1864. Note the hearse (carriage carrying a coffin), the Cavalry and the use of firearms by the mob.*

LONDON RIOTS 1886

This extract is from the *Graphic*, an illustrated magazine, for 13 February 1886:

> **The peace of the metropolis has been disturbed this week and property destroyed ... in a manner and to an extent unprecedented in the annals of modern London. A great demonstration of the unemployed in Trafalgar Square ... was made use of by leaders of the Revolutionary Social and Democratic Federation to [make] violent denunciations of the propertied classes. ... After a good deal of this incendiary speech-making, a large body of roughs, with the Social Democratic Leaders ... smashed the windows of the Carlton Club ... hurling missiles at passing carriages ... looting several shops...**

What words and phrases tell you that the journalist was angry about what had happened? The S.D.F. followed the teachings of Karl Marx. What does the encyclopaedia in your school library say about this important man?

21

The Mid-Nineteenth-Century Police

The first modern police force was set up in London in 1829 by the Home Secretary, Robert Peel. Acts of Parliament in 1835 and 1839 allowed towns and counties to set up similar forces, but it was not until 1856 that they were legally required to do so.

These rules were drawn up shortly after the ▶ founding of the Lancashire police force in 1839. Do you think these rules are still relevant for today's policemen?

THE METROPOLITAN POLICE FORCE

The *Quarterly Review* published this description of London's police force, the largest in Britain, in 1856:

> ...[It] consists of a Chief Commissioner, Sir Richard Mayne, 2 Assistant Commissioners... 18 Superintendents, 133 Inspectors, 625 Sergeants and 4954 Constables.... [The force] watches by night and day every alley, street, and square... tries every accessible door and window of London's 400,000 houses... exercises a surveillance over the 8000 reputed thieves... and keeps in awe the 40,000... people who form "the uneasy classes".... The entire district has an area of... 700 square miles, 100 of which... is covered... with brick and mortar.... This wide extent of ground is mapped out into 18 divisions...

Calculate the total strength of London's police force in 1856. What rank was held by the officers who commanded each division? What sort of people made up "the uneasy classes"?

COUNTY OF LANCASTER CONSTABULARY FORCE.

THE FOLLOWING MAXIMS
Are to be strictly observed and borne in mind by the Constables of the Force

1. Constables are placed in authority to PROTECT, not to OPPRESS, the PUBLIC.
2. To do which effectually, they must earnestly and systematically exert themselves to PREVENT CRIME.
3. When a Crime has been committed, no time should be lost, nor exertions spared, to discover and bring to justice the OFFENDERS.
4. Obtain a knowledge of all REPUTED THIEVES, and IDLE and DISORDERLY PERSONS.
5. Watch narrowly all Persons having NO VISIBLE MEANS OF SUBSISTENCE.
6. Prevent VAGRANCY.
7. Be IMPARTIAL in the discharge of duties.
8. Discard from the mind all POLITICAL and SECTARIAN prejudices.
9. Be COOL and INTREPID in the discharge of duties in emergencies and unavoidable conflicts.
10. Avoid ALTERCATIONS, and display PERFECT COMMAND of TEMPER under INSULT and gross PROVOCATION, to which all Constables must occasionally be liable.
11. NEVER STRIKE but in SELF-DEFENCE, nor treat a Prisoner with more Rigour than may be absolutely necessary to prevent escape.
12. Practice the most complete SOBRIETY, one instance of DRUNKENNESS will render a Constable liable to DISMISSAL.
13. Treat with the utmost CIVILITY all classes of HER MAJESTY'S SUBJECTS, and cheerfully render ASSISTANCE to all in need of it.
14. Exhibit DEFERENCE and RESPECT to the MAGISTRACY.
15. Promptly and cheerfully OBEY all SUPERIOR OFFICERS.
16. Render an HONEST, FAITHFUL, and SPEEDY account of all MONIES and PROPERTY, whether intrusted with them for others, or taken possession of in the execution of duty.
17. With reference to the foregoing, bear especially in mind that "HONESTY IS THE BEST POLICY."
18. Be perfectly neat and clean in Person and Attire.
19. Never sit down in a PUBLIC HOUSE or BEER SHOP.
20. AVOID TIPPLING.
21. It is the interest of every man to devote some portion of his spare time to the practice of READING and WRITING and the general improvement of his mind.
22. IGNORANCE is an insuperable bar to promotion.

J. WOODFORD
Chief Constable

A LACK OF CO-OPERATION

Mid-nineteenth-century police forces did not always work happily together. In Hampshire there was a county police force as well as separate forces in the five main towns. A parliamentary committee heard this story in 1853 from the Hampshire Chief Constable:

> ...one of the superintendents of the Hants constabulary was proceeding on duty from the Southampton terminus in plain clothes, when he saw in the train a desperate character, who a year and a half previously had effected his

THE SHEFFIELD POLICE FORCE

Pawson and Brailsford's *Guide to Sheffield* (1862) describes a typical town police force of the period:

> Under the management of an energetic Watch Committee and a most intelligent Chief Constable [the force] has become a well-trained and thoroughly efficient body. Besides the Chief Constable (Mr John Jackson), there are a warrant officer, five detective officers, two inspectors, five sub-inspectors, eleven sergeants, and 162 constables. The principal police office is at the Town Hall. There is also a station in Tenten Street. The annual cost of the police force is about £11,000,

By 1871 there were over 27,000 policemen in England, one for every 828 of the population. What was the police/population ratio for Sheffield in 1862? (The town's population in 1861 was 185,000.) Note that the total cost of England's police force in 1871 was £2,225,000.

The nineteenth-century police station at Farnborough in Kent, just within the area covered by the Metropolitan Police. Note the "blue lamp" outside the entrance.

THE FUNCTIONS OF THE POLICE

Max Schlesinger was a German visitor to London who wrote a book about what he saw, called *Saunterings In and About London* (1853):

> ...the police in England is essentially a force of safety, whose functions are limited to the prevention of crime and the apprehension of criminals.... There has not hitherto been a political department in Scotland Yard. The police... deals only with the vulgar sins, larceny, robbery, murder and forgery; it superintends the cleansing of the streets; it prevents the interruption of the street traffic, and it takes care of drunkards and of children that have strayed from their homes. But political opinions... are altogether without the sphere of the English police.... The London policeman is the stranger's friend.... If you lose your way, turn to the first policeman you meet...

> escape by violence from two constables of our force; the superintendent immediately seized him, and ... sent to the borough station to borrow a pair of handcuffs.... the loan of these was refused; "they had none to spare"...
> (*Report of the Parliamentary Committee to Consider the Expediency of Adopting a More Uniform System of Police in England and Wales, and in Scotland*, 1853)

Why do you think the borough police force acted in this unreasonable way?

What job did the police have in 1853 which they no longer have today?

Policemen's Lives

Two of the most famous lines written by W.G. Gilbert (1836-1911) appear in the operetta *Pirates of Penzance* (1879):

> When constabulary duty's to be done,
> The policeman's lot is not a happy one.

Life for a Victorian policeman was hard, and only at the end of Victoria's reign did working conditions begin to improve.

DUTY

Charles Booth, in his 17-volume work, *Life and Labour of the People in London*, published at the end of the nineteenth century, devoted some space to London's policemen:

> A policeman is liable to duty at any time in the 24 hours, but the time spent regularly on his beat is only eight hours ... being either two watches of four hours ... between 6 a.m. and 10 p.m., or one period of eight hours in the night....
>
> The hours on the beat do not ... include all the time ordinarily occupied, as a constable has to attend court ... and is expected to work up his cases, and on extraordinary occasions ... he may be kept on duty for extra hours ... the prolonged walking, even at the regulation pace, is wearying to the feet. The ordinary policeman must continually perambulate his beat....

What payment would a policeman get today if he worked longer than his normal hours? Can you think of a sad occasion in 1901 when London policemen would have had to line the streets?

CONDITIONS OF SERVICE

> Neither Sundays nor other public holidays are times of rest for the police.... One day off in 14 is allowed ... sergeants and constables have a week or 10 days, and inspectors 2 or 3 weeks leave annually.... In the Metropolitan force the pay at first is 24 shillings and rises to 37 shillings [per week] in eight years. Sergeants rise to 40 shillings.... Inspectors begin at 56 shillings.... In addition ... all are supplied with uniform clothing and boots....
>
> Candidates must be under 27 years of age, and, if married, must not have more than two children when joining. The standard of height is 5ft 9in.... The bulk of the recruits ... are countrymen ... to whom the wages ... appear wealth. (Charles Booth, *Life and Labour of the People in London*, volume IV)

Ask your careers teacher whether he or she has any information about the police force today. How do conditions compare with those of the 1890s?

KILMARNOCK POLICE FORCE. 1878.

INSPECTOR PEARMAN

John Pearman served in the army between 1845 and 1857, rising to the rank of Sergeant. He then joined the police, rising to the rank of Inspector. He was

> ... in charge of the men employed at Eton College and the Street, and here I remained until I tendered my resignation to the Chief Constable, being 62½ years of age. At the October *Quarter Sessions* [of 1881], I was granted a pension ... of £69.6s.8d. per year ... and was presented with a testimonial in vellum.... "To John Pearman.... We the inhabitants of Eton desire to convey to you ... our appreciation of the faithful manner [in which] you fulfilled [your] ... office, and beg your acceptance of the accompanying purse of money. That your future may be blessed with all the goods this world can afford is the sincere wish of the subscribers."
> (*Sergeant Pearman's Memoirs*, edited by the Marquess of Anglesey, 1968)

The Quarter Sessions were a criminal court, held four times a year, and presided over by local Justices of the Peace. Notice that it was the local magistrates who decided that Pearman should get a pension. A pension was not a retired policeman's right at this time.

◀ *The police force of a Scottish town. Can you pick out the sergeant and the three officers? Note the beards and the similarity of the uniforms worn by the constables to those worn today by policemen in England. Scottish policemen now wear flat caps.*

"ASK A POLICEMAN"

1. "CONSTABLE, THAT CARMAN HAS BEEN GROSSLY INSOLENT TO ME! I INSIST ON YOUR TAKING HIS NUMBER"
2. "CONSTABLE, THAT DEAD DOG HAS LAIN HERE FOR THREE DAYS. I INSIST ON YOUR REMOVING IT INSTANTLY!"
3. "CUSH'BLE, TRESH PAVEMENTS POSH'V'LY DANG'ROUS! I INSIST ON YOUR SETTING 'EM SHTRAIGHT!"
4. "OH! CONSTABLE, THOSE PEOPLE OPPOSITE ARE SOLD OUT OF CASHMERE AT ONE AND SEVENPENCE THREE-FARTHINGS A YARD! CAN YOU TELL ME WHERE TO GO?"

The Strand Magazine of August 1892 pokes fun at the silly demands the public makes of policemen.

"ROZZERS" OR "BOBBIES"?

Robert Roberts grew up in Salford not long after Queen Victoria's death. The people he knew did not regard the police in such a kindly way as the inhabitants of Eton:

> ... nobody in our Northern slum ... ever spoke in fond regard of the policeman ... like their children ... the poor in general looked upon him with fear and dislike.... Except for common narks [informers], one spoke to a "rozzer" when one had to and told him the minimum.... The middle and upper classes ... held their "bobby" in patronizing affection and esteem ... but these sentiments were never shared ... by the working class... (*The Classic Slum*, R. Roberts, 1971)

Can you explain the different views of the police which Roberts describes? How did Sir Robert Peel's name give rise to policemen being called "bobbies"? (They were called "peelers" in the 1830s.)

25

Courts, Judges and Sentences

A prisoner, once apprehended and charged, faced trial. Those accused of serious crimes were tried at the Old Bailey in London or the local County Court. Less serious crimes were dealt with by magistrates.

SENTENCING OF PRISONERS

The anonymous author of *The Great Metropolis* (1837), which describes scenes of London life, recounts the way in which prisoners were sentenced at the Old Bailey:

> They are sentenced in classes.... I have seen 50 or 60 poor creatures standing at the bar at the same time. And a more affecting spectacle ... is seldom witnessed.... I have seen the down-cast eye and the trembling frame of the prisoner who expected some severe punishment, succeeded ... by the most manifest tokens of joy, when the punishment to be inflicted was comparatively lenient.... on the other hand ... female prisoners.... [expecting] that they would get off with a few months imprisonment ... turn pale as death, look ... wildly about them, then close their eyes, and uttering a heart-rending shriek, fall down in a swoon, when the sentence of transportation for life has been passed upon them.

If you read the section of this book on "Transportation to Australia" you will understand why this punishment was regarded with such horror.

THE OLD BAILEY

Knight's Cyclopeadia of London (1851) contained the following description of the Central Criminal Court, popularly known as the "Old Bailey". On entering the court:

> The first sentiment is one of disappointment. The ... pre-eminence of the Court makes one ... anticipate a grander physical exhibition. What does meet our gaze is ... a square hall ... having on the left a gallery ... and on the right the bench ... with desks at intervals for the use of the judges, whilst in the body of the court are ... a dock for the prisoners below the gallery ... then, just in advance of the left hand corner of the dock, the circular witness-box, and, in a similarly relative position to the witness-box, the jury-box....

Draw a ground plan of the Old Bailey. Have you visited your local court? Perhaps your school can arrange a visit.

THE ROLE OF THE JUDGE

The Frenchman H. A. Taine visited England several times between 1861 and 1871. His observations were published in England under the title *Notes on England* (1885).

> ... "the principle of English law is, that a man must be held to be innocent till he has been proved to be guilty".... Contrary to the French rule, the prisoner may keep his mouth closed; he is not bound to incriminate himself ... when the judge pronounces sentence,

A trial at the Old Bailey (the Central Criminal Court in London) in 1872. Note the prisoner, the gas lamps and the barristers, and on the right, four members of the jury. How many jurymen would there be in the complete picture?

PORTLAND PRISON 1849

The following list names some of the convicts held in Portland Prison in 1849:

NAME	AGE	OFFENCE	WHERE	SENTENCE
James Hackett	21	Felony	Salford	7
John Taylor	20	Stealing a file and moneys	Leicester	7
John Brown	20	Larceny previous con.	C.C. Court	7
James Barker	47	Stealing fowls, 2 indicts.	Exeter	14
William Johnson	25	Setting fire to 2 stacks of straw	Stafford	20
James Sweeney	58	Uttering count coin P.C.	Caernarvon	15
George Williams	21	Burglary P.C.	C.C. Court	10
Francis Best	35	Housebreaking & Larceny	Worcester	15
John Henry	36	Uttering forged notes	Glasgow	20
Thomas Hartshorn	33	Robbery with violence P.C.	Liverpool	15
Samuel Laughton	22	Burglary, stealing silver spoons etc.	Nottingham	14
Thomas Robinson	23	Burglary and theft, 2 indict.	Maidstone	14
Martin Stone	22	House stealing	Dorchester	15
Richard Ashford	58	Stealing 3 lbs of pork P.C.	Exeter	10
John Dobson	28	Stealing money from the person P.C.	Stafford	14
Samuel Diggle	36	Burglary	Liverpool	15
George Goult	22	Robbery P.C.	Chelmsford	12

he does so with authority and with impartiality.... He weighs his words, translating his carefully formed opinion into clear language.... More than once I have thought that if Justice herself had a voice, she would speak them.... The prisoner at the bar cannot help bowing before such a power as this....

Remember that the judge gives the jury (made up of 12 citizens) guidance on points of law, and sums up the evidence. The jury decides on the prisoner's guilt or innocence; the judge then passes sentence. Do you think Taine is impressed by the English judicial system?

"P.C." means "previous conviction", "indict" means "indictments" (charges) and "C.C. Court" means "Central Criminal Court", London. Notice the severity of the sentences, the age of the convicts and the fact that they were sent to Portland Prison (near Weymouth in Dorset) from all over the country.

27

Prisons and Hulks

Prisons in the 1830s and 1840s were in a state of transition. By no means all the evils which reformers like John Howard and Elizabeth Fry had campaigned against in the late eighteenth and early nineteenth centuries had been removed in the 1830s, and the use of "hulks" (old vessels used as floating prisons) lasted until 1857. However, in 1842 the model prison at Pentonville was opened.

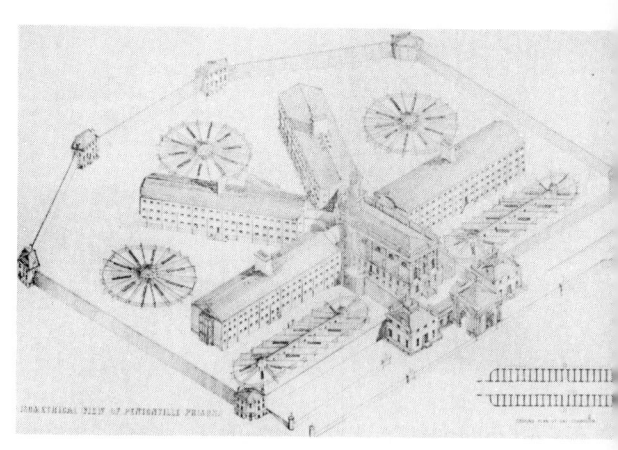

Study the above picture alongside the description of Pentonville Prison.

THE MODEL PRISON, PENTONVILLE

The first stone of the prison building was laid in April 1840.... It contains four radiating wings, with corridors running throughout, having cells on each side.... There are 1,000 cells, each of which is 13 feet long, 7 feet broad and 9 feet high.... Each is provided with a stone water-closet pan, a metal basin supplied with water, a three-legged stool, a small table, a shaded gas-burner, and a hammock, with mattress and blankets.... Each cell is warmed by hot air.... None of the prisoners are ever seen by each other.... The officers wear felted shoes, and can inspect the prisoners, whether in his cell or in the airing [exercise] yard, without being either heard or seen. Each prisoner is visited hourly during the day by a keeper... (Charles Knight, *The Cyclopaedia of London* 1851).

Pentonville was the first "modern" prison built in Britain, and subsequent ones were built to a similar design. Many of these are still in use today, although the "silent system" which was operated in the 1840s at Pentonville has long since been abandoned, for reasons explained in the next section of this book.

THE HULKS

John Wade (1788-1875) was a journalist and historian. In his 1829 *Treatise on the Police and Crimes of the Metropolis* he described the "hulk" system:

... the hulks are large vessels without masts, which have been ... battleships ... and are moored near a dock-yard, or arsenal, so that the labour of the convicts may be applied to the public service. The present establishment consists of 10 vessels.... The principal stations are at Deptford, Woolwich, Chatham, Sheerness and Portsmouth.... [The convicts] are sent out in gangs ... to work on shore, guarded by soldiers.

By the late 1850s sufficient modern prisons had been built for these floating prisons to be broken up.

London's prisons in 1851. This illustration is from Knight's Cyclopaedia of London, 1851. There were in fact thirteen prisons in London at this time. ▶

NEWGATE

William Thornbury, author of *Old and New London* (1880), ended his description of Newgate, the famous London prison, by saying:

> **Even in 1836 the Inspector of Prisons found fault with the system within the prison. The prisoners were allowed to amuse themselves with gambling, card-playing, and draughts; sometimes they obtained, by stealth ... the luxury of tobacco, and a newspaper. Instruments to facilitate prison-breaking were found in the prison. Combs and towels were not provided, and the supply of soap was not sufficient.**

Try to find out about the work of John Howard and Elizabeth Fry. Most encyclopaedias will have entries on them.

THE CLOSURE OF PRISONS FOR DEBTORS

The Gentleman's Magazine in 1842 noted that:

> **The Fleet and Marshalsea Prisons have been closed during the past month. There were 70 prisoners in the Fleet, and only 3 in the Marshalsea; and their removal took place to the Queen's Prison ... some of the prisoners had been confined a very long time.... [One] eccentric character, named Jeremiah Board, had been an inmate of the Fleet 28 years.... The total number of prisoners for debt in London may now be stated at about 760. Some years ago there were as many in one prison.**

Why do you think debtors were held in prison? Is imprisonment a suitable way of dealing with people who do not pay their debts?

29

The Separate and Silent Systems

In the 1830s and 1840s prison reformers argued over the relative effectiveness of two particular methods of punishing and reforming prisoners, and deterring others from crime.

THE SEPARATE SYSTEM

At London's Pentonville prison in the 1840s, inmates served the first 18 months of their sentence under the "separate system" (see page 28). The theory behind this was explained by a prison chaplain as follows:

> Some argue that it is very unnatural to isolate men and seclude them in separate cells, but it is not more unkind, than to isolate an individual with the plague, and keep him under medical treatment, until the contagion [disease] shall have been removed, and the individual be fit to resume the duties of life. (R.V. Reynolds, *The Outcasts of England*, 1850)

In fact the system had to be radically altered as many of the Pentonville prisoners went mad as a result of their near total isolation. The period of solitary confinement before transportation or transfer to one of the convict prisons (such as Dartmoor) was reduced to 12 months in 1848, to nine months in 1853, and to 6 months in 1899.

THE SILENT SYSTEM

The Reverend John Clay was also a prison Chaplain. In his report for 1838 he described the "silent system" and explained the thinking behind it:

> [It] permits the employment of prisoners in sight of each other, but forbids the slightest degree of intercourse [contact] by words, signs or looks, and provides for complete separation at night. This system is asserted to possess one superior quality among others – the placing of men under trying circumstances where they are compelled to exercise, and many acquire, the valuable habit of self-control. At the same time ... it exacts respect to authority, order, cleanliness, decency at meals, and industry and labour.

Why do you think so many prison chaplains wrote books about crime and prisons? Do you think it would be difficult not to talk to anyone all day?

(Below left) The separate system, Pentonville chapel. You can see a similar chapel at Lincoln Castle, which was used as a prison in Victoria's reign.
(Below) The silent system, Millbank workshop.

PICKING OAKUM

Henry Mayhew and John Binney, in their book *The Criminal Prisons of London* (1862), described the silent system operating in the oakum-picking room of a prison.

> **The building was full of men, and as silent as if it merely contained so many automota, for the only sound heard was like that of the rustling of a thicket, or ... the ticking of clock-work – something resembling that heard, in a ... clockmaker's shop, where hundreds of time-pieces are going together.**
>
> **The utter absence of noise struck us as being absolutely terrible. The silence seemed ... almost intense enough to hear a flake of snow fall.**

Prisons operated a rule of silence for the rest of the nineteenth century. Can you imagine any of the ways the prisoners tried to get round this rule? "Oakum" is the loose fibre obtained by unpicking and untwisting old rope. It is used for plugging the gaps between ships' timbers.

PORTLAND PRISON

On Sunday 20 August 1882 Mary Gladstone (daughter of the Prime Minister, W.E. Gladstone) visited Portland Prison and recorded her observations in her diary:

> **Went all over the place ... the dining [arrangements] perhaps the most striking of all. A loaf and cheese stood on the floor in front of 250 cells. At the word of command the doors opened as if by magic and 250 convicts stood on the thresholds. "Pick up your dinners." They all stooped. "Back to your cells. Shut your doors," and with a crash of thunder they all vanished and every door was double locked. They may never speak to each other. They lose all identity and are only known by the numbers on their backs.**

How would you describe this young woman's reactions to life in this prison?

Pentonville Prison in 1845. All English prisons built after Pentonville employed the cell system. Solitary confinement was seen as beneficial because it isolated a prisoner from the bad influence of other prisoners and provided an opportunity for "that calm contemplation which brings repentance".

Transportation to Australia

1987 was the two hundreth anniversary of the first landing of convicts in Australia. After eight months at sea, 11 ships, carrying 736 convicts, sailed into Botany Bay (near present-day Sydney). In the years between 1787 and 1868, when transportation was finally abolished, many thousands of convicts were sent to Australia. Transportation was meant both as a punishment and as a way of ridding Britain of undesirable men and women.

AN IMPUDENT IRISHMAN

This story is from *The Great Metropolis*, published anonymously in 1837.

> [An] Irishman, on being sentenced to transportation for life ... turned back ... and looking the judge ... in the face, said, "Will your honour allow me to speak one word?"
>
> "Certainly", said the judge, thinking he was about to make a confession of the crime of which he had been found guilty.
>
> "Well then, your honour, it's myself will be happy to carry out letters to any of your honour's friends in Botany Bay."
>
> "Take him away", said the judge...

Why do you think the judge was not amused by this?

FOURTEEN YEARS' TRANSPORTATION

Henry Mayhew once interviewed a man who had been arrested for passing three forged £5 notes:

> I was sentenced to 14 years transportation. I was ten weeks in the *Bellerophon* hulk at Sheerness, and was then taken to Hobart Town, Van Diemen's Land [Tasmania], in the *Sir Godfrey Webster*.... [When we arrived] the settlers came from all parts and picked their men out.... [After] twelve years service ... my time was up but I had incurred several punishments.... The first was 25 lashes, because a bag of flour had been burst, and I picked up a capful.... In all I had 875 lashes at my different punishments. I used to boast of it at last.

Why did the settlers "pick out" convicts? In view of the brutal punishments this man received in Australia it is not surprising that Mayhew tells us that he looked older than his 43 years.

THE NUMBERS TRANSPORTED

The *Judicial Statistics* for 1857 contained the following table, showing the number of convicts transported to Australia in the years 1787-1857:

	Males.	Females.	Total.
From 1787 to 1796 ..	3,792	865	4,657
,, 1797 ,, 1806 ..	2,568	813	3,381
,, 1807 ,, 1816 ..	4,390	1,252	5,642
,, 1817 ,, 1826 ..	16,750	1,472	18,222
,, 1827 ,, 1836 ..	32,780	4,337	37,117
,, 1837 ,, 1846 ..	23,550	3,708	27,258
,, 1847 ,, 1856 ..	10,241	1,736	11,977
In the Year 1857	461	..	461
Total	94,532	14,183	108,715

About 5000 convicts were sent to Western Australia in the nine years after 1857. Draw a bar chart showing the number of convicts transported in each ten-year period between 1787 and 1856. Try to find out why transportation was used as a means of punishing criminals – even those convicted of what we would call trivial offences.

CONVICTS AT WORK

The treatment of convicts in Australia varied, as these extracts from the 1837 Select Committee on Transportation make clear:

> The condition ... of by far the most numerous class of convicts, those who are employed, as shepherds or neatherds [cowherds], and in agriculture generally, is undoubtedly inferior to that of a convict, who is either a domestic servant, or a mechanic [a skilled craftsman]; they are, however ... better fed, than the generality of agricultural labourers in England...

However, those convicts who stole or got drunk (about 1700 in the 1830s) found themselves

> employed in making roads in New South Wales and Van Diemen's Land... they are kept at work under a strict military guard during the day, and liable to suffer flagellation [flogging] for trifling offences ... being in chains, discipline is more easily preserved ... and escape more easily prevented...

If you read *Oliver Twist* by Charles Dickens you will find that the character called the Artful Dodger was sentenced to transportation.

"AUSTRALIA AS IT IS"

First published in 1867 in London, *Australia As It Is* describes many aspects of life "down under". In the chapter entitled "Conviction", the author, a clergyman, remarks that:

PENAL SETTLEMENTS

Convicts in Australia who committed serious crimes (there were about 2500 in this category in the late 1830s) were re-transported to settlements such as Norfolk Island. This was a small volcanic island, situated 1000 miles from the eastern shores of Australia. Conditions were so harsh that the 1837 Molesworth Committee was told of

> the case of several men cutting off the heads of their fellow prisoners with a hoe while at work, with a certainty ... of being executed ... but it was better than being where they were.

Locate on a map the various places mentioned in this section on transportation.

> There can be no doubt whatever of the material advantages ... which transportation [gave] to a large number of criminals. They were placed in a much better position than they would have been in Great Britain and Ireland for acquiring wealth and independence. Many of them never served out their sentences; good behaviour was rewarded by a ticket-of-leave, and they were entirely free to dispose of their labour to their own best advantage.

Most convicts stayed on in Australia after they had served their sentences. Why do you think this was? The ticket-of-leave system was introduced in Britain in 1853; it permitted long-sentence men to complete their sentences outside prison, subject to recall if they broke the conditions of their release (reporting periodically to a police station for instance). Do you know what we call the similar system that operates today?

Dartmoor Prison

Dartmoor is one of our most famous prisons. It was one of a number of "convict stations" opened in the late 1840s, in response to growing opposition from reformers to transportation and the use of hulks. Other "convict stations" were set up at Chatham, Portland and Portsmouth.

THE CLIMATE ON DARTMOOR

Murray's Handbook to Devon and Cornwall (1872) quoted a Monsieur Cartel who had been a prisoner of war at Dartmoor in the early nineteenth century:

> For seven months in the year it is a "vraie Siberie" [true Siberia], covered with unmelting snows. When the snows go away, the mists appear. Imagine the tyranny of "perfide Albion" [wicked England] in sending human beings to such a place!

Captain V. Harris, however, a one-time governor of the prison, painted a different picture, in his book *Dartmoor Prison, Past and Present* (1888):

> A large proportion [of the convicts] are sent to Dartmoor for their health's sake, for, in the early stages of chest complaint, the climate is most efficacious [helpful]. The medical officers have ... recorded ... the improved conditions of men removed from London and the large manufacturing towns...

Can you explain why these two accounts differ so much? The final extract in this section may suggest the real reason why the health of some convicts improved.

"PARCERE SUBJECTIS"

White's Directory of Devon, 1878-9 gave a description of Dartmoor Prison, which had originally been built in 1809 to hold French and American prisoners of war:

> [It] now consists of five rectangular buildings, each 300 feet [91m] long by fifty feet [15m] broad and the entrance is arched over with immense blocks of granite, on which is engraved the appropriate inscription "Parcere Subjectis". A considerable addition [to the buildings] has recently been added by the labour of the convicts... who are sent here for 5 years and upwards. They are divided into three classes, distinguished by a strip of black, yellow or blue cloth on the collar of the jacket...

The Latin inscription can be translated as "Show mercy to those who are conquered". The words come from Virgil's poem, the *Aeneid* and educated men in Victorian times, who were brought up on the "Classics", would have recognized them.

Convicts in the late nineteenth century at work ▶ (perhaps digging a drainage ditch) on Dartmoor. Note the warder's rifle and the uniforms worn by the convicts.

AN ATTEMPTED ESCAPE

"Ticket-of-leave man", the anonymous author of *Convicts Life* (1879), described how:

> We had stacked our rakes and forks, so that we were entirely unarmed, and three officers armed with loaded rifles were in charge of us. We were unwisely allowed to go alone to the hedge, which was at a considerable distance, to fetch our clothes. "Now is our chance!" said Morgan, and over the hedge went the conspirators. As I was one who remained behind I could take stock of the officers in charge.... I never saw men so completely taken off their guard.

These men may have surprised the warders but they did not get very far. At Dartmoor there was a reward of £3 to anyone arresting an escaped convict. On this occasion 30 or 40 Devonshire labourers heard the signal gun and joined in the hunt. If you have ever been to Dartmoor or a similar moorland area you will understand why it was difficult for convicts to make a successful escape.

◀ *These small stones mark the graves of convicts who died at Dartmoor between 1851 and 1902. Why do you think the convicts did not get proper grave stones?*

HARD LABOUR

The anonymous author of *A Gentleman's Walking Tour of Dartmoor* (1864) described some of the work done by the convicts:

> The prisoners are chiefly employed on the farm, some in the actual cultivation of it, others in extending it.... At the latter occupation, they work in gangs, first raising all the surface stone... with which they build... walls.... They then clear the peat... in which... nothing will grow. They then drain, level and prepare for potatoes.... A considerable gang of convicts is employed in the quarries raising granite for the enclosure walls...

Some Victorians believed that "hard labour" should consist of pointless and painful work. Others believed that on financial as well as moral grounds the work ought to be productive. Which argument would you have supported?

Capital Punishment

The ultimate penalty for crime was death, and until the penal system was reformed by Sir Robert Peel (in the 1820s) and Lord John Russell (in the 1830s) many crimes against property, including the theft of goods worth more than £2, were punishable in this manner. After 1841, however, no one was executed in Great Britain except for murder.

A FALL IN EXECUTIONS

The *Quarterly Review* in October 1874 described changes in the law over the previous 50 years:

> ... our criminal code, instead of being almost Draconian [very severe], now verges on the opposite extreme.... In the 7 years ending 1820, 7107 persons were sentenced to death, of whom 649 were executed; in the following seven years, 7952 were so sentenced, of whom 494 were executed, and in the 7 years ending with 1834, 8483 persons were condemned to die, of whom 355 were executed; whilst in the seven years ending 1871, only 140 persons were sentenced to death, of whom 59 were executed.

In 1846 only six people were executed, and in 1849 66 people were sentenced to death, of whom 15 were executed. Plot the number of executions for the years mentioned in the extract above in the form of a graph or bar-chart. You could do the same for the number of death sentences. The number of executions fell as the number of crimes punishable by death was reduced. What alternative punishment do you think people convicted of serious crimes suffered?

Note the three policemen trying to keep order as the crowd awaits an execution in 1849.

THE DEATH SENTENCE

Arthur Morrison, a journalist, wrote a novel about life in the East End of London called *A Child of the Jago* (1896). In it he describes a murder trial:

> "Gentlemen of the jury, have you agreed upon your verdict?"
> "We have".
> "Do you find the prisoner at the bar guilty, or not guilty?"
> "Guilty"....
> The judge ... arranged ... on his head ... a sort of soft mortarboard ... with a large silk tassel hanging over the side....
> "Joshua Perret, you have been convicted ... of the horrible crime of wilful murder.... It is my duty to pronounce sentence of that punishment which ... the law of the country imposes.... The sentence of the Court is: that you be taken to the place whence you came, and thence to a place of execution; and that you be there Hanged by the Neck till you be Dead: and may the Lord have mercy on your soul!"

What are the arguments for and against the death penalty? The death penalty for murder was abolished in Great Britain in 1965.

A MACABRE REQUEST

The last public hanging in Cornwall was carried out in August 1862 at Bodmin. The man who was hanged by Calcraft, Cornwall's "well known and expert hangman", was 28-year-old John Doidge. He had murdered another man who had taken his job after he, Doidge, had been sacked. The day after the execution the local newspaper, *The West Briton* carried this strange story:

> Two women presented themselves at the gaol in the early morning of Monday; their request was that they might be allowed, as a cure for sore necks, to be touched by the convict's hand, after his death by hanging!

THE CROWD

Executions took place in public until 1868. Public hangings were popular occasions, though some people like Charles Dickens campaigned against them. In the mid-nineteenth century the Great Western Railway even offered cheap excursion tickets to see London executions. Thomas Miller, in his *Picturesque Sketches of London* (1852), described one scene outside Newgate Prison:

> Hush! the unceasing murmer of the mob now breaks into a loud deep roar.... the wide, dark sea of heads is all at once in motion... each... sees, coiled upon the floor of the scaffold, like a serpent, the hangman's rope! The loud shout of the multitude once more subsided... then followed sounds more distinct... in which ginger beer, pies, fried fish, sandwiches and fruit were vended.... Another fight followed the score [large number] which had already taken place; this time 2 women were the combatants.... Another deep roar, louder than any which had preceded it, broke from the multitude. Then came the cry of "Hats off!".... It was followed by the deep and solemn booming of the death bell from the church of St Sepulchre.

Why do you think executions were carried out in public? Local newspapers carried detailed reports of executions even after 1868.

A LETTER FROM DICKENS

On 14 November 1849 *The Times* published a letter from Charles Dickens:

> I was a witness of the execution at Horsemonger-lane this morning. I went there with the intention of observing the crowd.... A sight so inconceivably awful as the wickedness and levity [silliness] of the immense crowd... could be imagined by no man.... The horrors of the gibbet [gallows] and of the crime which brought the wretched murderers to it, faded in my mind before the atrocious bearing, looks and language of the assembled spectators ... thieves, low prostitutes, ruffians and vagabonds of every kind.... I do not believe that any community can prosper where such a scene of horror and demoralization... is... presented...

Clearly, Dickens thought public executions were degrading and harmful. Can you explain why so many people enjoyed going to these spectacles?

Law and Order in the West Country

Victorian local newspapers are a valuable source of information on crime and punishment. These extracts are from three West Country newspapers but you will find that the nineteenth-century local newspapers in your area reported similar stories.

PLYMOUTH MAGISTRATES' COURT

On 3 September 1853 the *Plymouth, Devonport and Stonehouse Herald* described some of the cases recently tried by the local magistrates:

> **A dirty looking fellow, named Francis Wall, was accused of disorderly conduct.... The Bench [the magistrates] administered an admonition.... Susan Webber, one of the unfortunate class [she was probably a prostitute]... was charged with pocket-picking.... The Bench cautioned Webber as to the consequences of the unhappy life she was now leading. She was then discharged. Garden Robbing – John Harvey, an errand boy... was accused of.... stealing apples.... The Mayor said he had no doubt the lad was sorry at being caught, but... offences of this nature were now of such frequent occasion... [that] it was almost useless for any inhabitant to grow flowers or fruit...**

Harvey was sent to prison for seven days. If you look through your present-day local paper you will find that similar cases are still tried by magistrates. Children, however are not now sent to prison.

CORNWALL ASSIZES 1853

The *Plymouth, Devonport and Stonehouse Herald* carried reports on the more serious cases tried at the county court. On 30 July 1853 the paper told how

> **James Hart, a boy 10 years old, was indicted for putting stones on the West Cornwall Railway, with intent to obstruct engines etc.... When called upon to plead, the boy said: "Indeed Sir, I did not mean to do no harm. I did not know it was any harm...." The jury found the prisoner guilty, but recommended him to mercy on the grounds of his youth – six months' imprisonment, hard labour.**

Railways were still a novelty in Cornwall in 1853, and Hart may genuinely not have realized that his actions could have led to a derailment. The punishment was intended to be lenient. Do you think it was?

38

◀ The main entrance to Bodmin Gaol. Public executions, 51 in total, were carried out in front of the gateway from the 1770s to the 1860s.

A view of Bodmin Gaol as it is today. It was built in the 1770s, enlarged in the mid-nineteenth century and continued in use until 1922. In the later nineteenth century the prison held naval, as well as civil, prisoners. ▶

AN EXECUTION

An execution at Bodmin Gaol on 13 November 1882 was described as follows in the *Cornish Guardian*, published in Liskeard.

> Bodmin, Monday 9.15 a.m. The convict William Meager Bartlett was executed this morning at 8 o'clock in the presence of the Under Sheriff and the prison officials. The black flag was hoisted at one minute past 8 o'clock. The proceedings were strictly private. Marwood was the executioner and there was not the least struggle, death being instantaneous.... Bartlett was visited yesterday by his cousin and brother-in-law ... he confessed that he had killed the child and that he was prepared to meet his fate.

Compare this account with that of the public execution on page 37. Notice that our Victorian forefathers liked to read all about a condemned man's last days. Do you think today's newspapers would carry such details if we still had the death sentence?

JUVENILE CULPRITS FLOGGED

This story was carried in the *West Briton*, published in Truro, on 9 January 1868:

> On Thursday four boys named Henry Guest, Henry Bailey, William Trelease and J. Downing, charged with breaking into a brewery, and stealing some beer, were sentenced as follows: Guest and Bailey, 12 lashes each; Trelase 9, and Downing, 6 lashes.... On Friday evening the sentences... [were] carried out by P.C. Prater, in the presence of the Mayor, the Magistrate, and the Superintendent of Police.

Why did the flogging have to be carried out in the presence of the people named in the last sentence of the extract? What arguments might be made for and against the re-introduction of flogging for football hooligans and similar offenders?

Broadsheets and the Yellow Press

Up until the 1860s, "broadsheets" (sheets of paper with songs and stories printed on one side) were important to the ordinary people as a cheap source of entertainment. In the second half of Victoria's reign their place was taken by cheap newspapers, magazines and mass-produced books.

CONSTANCE KENT

These extracts are from a broadsheet ballad of 1865.

> Oh give attention, you maidens dear,
> My dying moments are drawing near,
> When I am sentenced alas to die
> Upon a gallows gloomy and high.
>
> My little brother, a darling sweet,
> That fatal moment did soundly sleep,
> I was perplexed. I invented strife,
> Fully determined to take his life.

There are ten other verses. Kent was not in fact executed. She was reprieved, served 20 years in prison and in 1885 emigrated to Canada. Can you suggest why she was reprieved?

A story from The Illustrated Police News, *5 October 1867. A publican and his wife tried to rob and murder a guest. The police arrived in the nick of time.*

HENRY'S DOWNFALL

The following song seems to have been popular in both Britain and Australia in the nineteenth century. Henry goes poaching and is caught:

> Come all you wild and wicked youths
>   wherever you may be,
> I pray you give attention and listen unto
>   me.
>
> It was at the March assizes we then did
>   repair,
> Like Job we stood with patience to hear
>   our sentence there,
> There being some old offences, which
>   made our case go bad,
> My sentence was for 14 years.
>
> The ship that bore us from the land, the
>   "Speedwell" was her name,
> For full five months and upwards, boy,
>   we ploughed the foaming main.
>
> I often looked behind me towards my
>   native shore,
> The cottage of contentment that I never
>   shall see more,
> Nor yet my own dear father who tore
>   his hoary hair,
> Likewise my tender mother, the womb
>   that did me bear.

You can read the rest of the ballad, and others like it, in *Old Bush Songs*, and in *The Oxford Book of English Traditional Verse* (see page 47).

This illustration accompanied the story about the ▶ *"Dreadful Murder at a Bank!".*

THE POPULAR PRESS

Max Schlesinger noted in his *Saunterings In and About London* (1853) how the British lapped up tales of sensational crimes, portrayed in publications like *The Penny Illustrated Paper*.

> **A criminal process, robbery and murder, a case of poisoning – these suffice to keep ... families ... in breathless suspense for weeks. ... The daily and weekly newspapers cannot find space enough for all the details ... woe to the paper that dared to curtail these interesting reports! It would at once lose its supporters.**

Do you think people still yearn for something that will make their flesh creep when they read a newspaper today?

"DREADFUL MURDER AT A BANK!"

This is a typical story from the Victorian magazine *The Illustrated Police News* of 15 July 1871. The magazine printed lurid stories and pictures of murders and suicides, not just in Britain but throughout the world.

> **The cashier of the Northern Bank at Newtonstewart, County Tyrone, Ireland, has been murdered, and the bank robbed of its cash, the unfortunate man having been discovered ... on Thursday afternoon, lying beside the open safe ... his skull having been beaten in. ...**
>
> **No trace has yet been discovered which can lead to the detection of the murderer but every effort is being made to find him out.**

Victorian Detective Novels

The Criminal Investigation Department of the Metropolitan Police had its origins in the "plain clothes" detectives first appointed in 1842. However, London's C.I.D. was not set up until 1878, and its failure to solve the "Jack the Ripper" murders in 1888 demonstrated its shortcomings. In fiction, nonetheless, the detective rapidly became a popular and successful figure.

SERGEANT CLUFF

Wilkie Collins's novel *The Moonstone* (1868) is often described as the first detective story. Cluff has the job of investigating the theft of a valuable jewel from Lady Verinder.

> A fly [a light carriage] drove up [to] ... the lodge, and out got a grizzled, elderly man, so miserably lean that he looked as if he had not got an ounce of flesh on his bones.... He was dressed ... in black.... His face was as sharp as a hatchet, and the skin of it was as yellow and dry and withered as an autumn leaf. His eyes ... had a very disconcerting trick, when they encountered your eyes, of looking as if they expected something more from you than you were aware of yourself. His walk was soft; his voice was melancholy.... He might have been a parson ... [or] an undertaker....
> "Is this Lady Verinder's?" he asked.
> "Yes, Sir!"
> "I am Sergeant Cluff".

Cluff was based on a real detective, Sergeant Whicher, who was involved in the Constance Kent case in the 1860s (see page 40).

SHERLOCK HOLMES

Arthur Conan Doyle's Sherlock Holmes is the most famous of all Victorian fictional detectives. In 1892 Holmes was involved in 'The Adventure of Silver Blaze', a short story concerning the disappearance of a racehorse and the murder of its trainer. Dr Watson here describes his journey to Exeter with Holmes:

> ... Sherlock Holmes, with his sharp, eager face framed in his earflapped travelling cap.... offered me his cigar case.
> "We are going well", said he, looking out of the window, and glancing at his watch. "Our rate at present is fifty-three and a half miles an hour".
> "I have not observed the quarter-mile posts", said I.
> "Nor have I, but the telegraph posts upon this line are sixty yards apart, and the calculation is a simple one..."

Do you understand how Holmes worked out the speed of the train? Conan Doyle wrote many short stories about Sherlock Holmes, as well as four full-length novels. If you have not read them, then you have a treat in store!

THE MAN WHO WAS HOLMES

It seems likely that Conan Doyle based his detective on Dr Joseph Bell, under whom Doyle studied at Edinburgh University. Bell had an extraordinary skill in diagnosis. On one occasion a woman with a small child came to his surgery. At a glance, Bell was able to deduce that she had set out that morning with two children, that she worked in a linoleum factory, lived in Burntisland (on the opposite side of the Firth of Forth to Edinburgh) and had come to Bell's rooms via Inverleigh Row:

THE MYSTERY OF A HANSOM CAB

This book, by Fergus Hume, was the most popular crime novel of the nineteenth century, outselling even Conan Doyle. It was written, set and published in Melbourne, Australia. One night a driver finds a corpse, reeking of chloroform gas, in his cab:

> "Well," said Mr Gorby, addressing his reflection in the looking glass, "I've been finding out things these last twenty years, but this is a puzzler and no mistake!" ... The hansom cab murder had been put into his hands ... and he was trying to think of how to make a beginning.
> "Hang it ... a thing with an end must have a start, and if I don't get the start how am I to get the end?"

This novel has been reprinted in paperback by The Hogarth Press. See if your local library has a copy, and find out how Gorby solved the mystery.

This is one of Sidney Paget's original illustrations for The Adventure of Silver Blaze. *Dr Watson sits facing Sherlock Holmes, who is wearing the famous "deer-stalker" hat.*

INSPECTOR BUCKETT

One of the characters in Dickens's *Bleak House* (1853) is the "sagacious, indefatigable detective officer", Mr Inspector Buckett.

> As they walk along, Mr Snagsby observes ... that however quick their pace may be, his companion [Buckett] still seems to lurk and lounge; also, that whenever he is going to turn to the right or left, he pretends to have a fixed purpose in his mind of going straight ahead, and wheels off, sharply, at the very last moment. Now and then when they pass a police-constable on his beat ... both appear entirely to overlook each other, and to gaze into space...

Can you explain why Buckett acted as he did?

> You see, gentlemen, when she said good morning to me I noticed her Fife accent, and ... the nearest town in Fife is Burntisland. ... [She had] red clay on the edges ... of her shoes the only such clay [in the area] is in the Botanical gardens. Inverleigh Row borders the gardens and is her nearest way here. ... the coat she carried ... is too big for the child who is with her and therefore she set out ... with two children. Finally, she had a dermatitis on ... her right hand which is peculiar to the workers in the linoleum factory at Burntisland.
> (*The Lancet*, 1 August 1956)

Map

Difficult Words

affray	a breach of the peace caused by fighting in a public place.
aggravate	increase the gravity of, for example, an assault.
almanack	a calendar of days and months, usually with astronomical information.
assizes	a law court.
chaplain	a clergyman working for a particular organization.
charivari	hurly-burly, commotion.
Chartists	people in the years 1838-48 who wanted working men to have the vote.
chloroform	a liquid used as an anaesthetic in nineteenth-century medecine.
constabulary	a police force.
cudgel	a thick stick used as a weapon.
curate	the assistant priest of a parish.
fence	someone who buys stolen goods from a thief.
guildhall	a town hall.
hoary	grey with age.
impartial	fair.
indefatigable	unwearying; unremitting.
industry	hard work.
Justice of the Peace (J.P.)	a magistrate; an unpaid judge who tries minor offences.
juvenile	a young person.
lenient	not severe.
mart	a shop.
maxim	a rule.
(the) metropolis	London.
off-licence	a shop licensed by the local magistrate to sell alcohol.
operetta	a short opera in one act.
penitentiary	prison.
perambulate	walk up and down.
proletariat	the working class of the towns.
quarter-staff	a stout pole (about 2½ metres in length) used as a weapon.
reformatory	a prison-like institution for young criminals.
sagacious	wise.
temperance	avoidance of excessive drinking of alcohol, or complete abstinence from drinking alcohol.

CONVERSION TABLE

NEW MONEY		OLD MONEY
1p	=	2.4d. (2.4 old pence)
5p	=	1s. (1 shilling)
50p	=	10s. (10 shillings)
£1	=	£1
		12d=1 shilling
		20 shillings=£1
£1.05	=	21 shillings (a guinea)

Date List

1829 Metropolitan Police established.
1834 The "silent system" first introduced into an English prison.
1835 Prisons Act; the first prison inspectors appointed. Municipal Corporations Act gave boroughs the power to set up their own police forces.
1837 Victoria succeeded to the throne.
1838 Parkhurst Prison opened for juvenile offenders.
1839 End of Bow Street Runners.
1839 City of London Police set up.
1839 County Police Act; allowed local J.P.s to establish police forces in the counties.
1839 Metropolitan Police boundaries extended to 15 miles from Charing Cross.
1840 First use of detectives by the Metropolitan Police.
1842 Pentonville Prison opened as a new National Penitentiary.
1848 Portland Convict Prison opened.
1850 Portsmouth and Dartmoor Convict Prisons opened.
1852 Chatham Convict Prison opened.
1853 Transportation to Van Diemen's Land (Tasmania) ended.
1856 County and Borough Police Act; local J.Ps and boroughs ordered to set up police forces in their respective areas.
1857 Hulks discontinued. Act establishes county police forces in Scotland.
1864 Penal servitude (punishment by hard work) introduced as an alternative to transportation.
1867 Last transport sailed with convicts for Australia.
1868 Last public hanging.
1869 The Metropolitan Police began a register of habitual criminals.
1870 Police helmets, modelled on the spiked helmet worn by the German army, introduced.
1870 Prevention of Crimes Act; the photographing of prisoners compulsory.
1877 Prison Act; local gaols brought under government control.
1878 Criminal Investigation Department of Metropolitan Police formed out of the old Detective Branch.
1888 "Jack the Ripper" murders.
1889 Photography used to identify criminals.
1898 Treadwheel and crank discontinued.
1901 Police use bicycles.
1903 Queen Victoria died.
1908 Borstal Act; separate prisons set up for young male offenders between the ages of 16 and 21.

Book List

Modern Books
(Those written especially for children are marked by an asterisk)

Chesney, K., *The Victorian Underworld*, Maurice Temple Smith, 1970
Emsley, C., *Crime and Society in England 1750-1900*, Longmans, 1987
*Hopkins, A. and Macpherson G., *Law and Order*, Macdonald, 1985
Hughes, R., *The Fatal Shore*, Collins, 1987
*O'Neill, J., *Transported to Van Diemen's Land*, Cambridge, 1977
Priestly, P., *Victorian Prison Lives: English Prison Biography 1830-1914*, Methuen, 1985
*Searby, P., *The Chartists*, Longmans, 1967
*Searby, P., *The Chartists in Wales*, Longmans, 1986
*Speed, P.F., *Police and Prisons*, Longmans, 1986
Tobias, J.J. (ed.), *Nineteenth-Century Crime: Prevention and Punishment*, David and Charles, 1972

Tobias, J.J., *Crime and Industrial Society in the Nineteenth Century*, Penguin, 1972

*Wilkes J., *London Police in the Nineteenth Century*, Cambridge, 1977

Contemporary Books, Magazines and Newspapers

Your local reference library will have nineteenth-century local newspapers and magazines like the *Illustrated London News* and *The Times*. It will also have Victorian guide books for your area. All of these will provide information to help you build up a picture for yourself of Victorian law and order. You may also find that there are collections of local documents available. For example, Kent County Records Office has produced *Kentish Sources IV: Crime and Punishment*, edited by E. Melling (1969).

Novels

Dates of publication indicate the latest editions.

Collins, W., *The Moonstone*, Oxford, 1982
Collins, W., *The Woman in White*, Oxford, 1980
Conan Doyle, A. *The Adventures of Sherlock Holmes, The Hound of the Baskervilles, The Memoirs of Sherlock Holmes, The Sign of Four, A Study in Scarlet*, which are all published in many editions
Dickens, C., *Bleak House*, Penguin, 1980
Dickens, C., *Great Expectations*, Penguin, 1983
Dickens, C., *Oliver Twist*, Penguin, 1985
Hume, F., *The Mystery of a Hansome Cab*, Hogarth, 1985
Morrison, A., *A Child of the Jago*, Brydell Press, 1985

Sources of Extracts

(a) *Social Investigators of the Nineteenth Century*

Engels F., *The Condition of the Working Class in England*, 1892
Hollingshead, J., *Ragged London in 1861*, Dent, 1986
Fried, A. and Elman, R.M., *Charles Booth's London*, Penguin, 1971
Mayhew, H., *London Labour and the London Poor*, (volumes I, II, III and IV) William Kimber, 1950

(b) *Journals and Magazines*
The Graphic; The Illustrated London News; The Illustrated Police News; The Quarterly Review; The Strand Magazine.

(c) *Autobiographies and Diaries*
Anglesey, The Marquis of (ed.), *Sergeant Pearman's Memoirs*, J. Cape, 1961
Butler, S. (ed.), *A Gentleman's Walking Tour of Dartmoor*, Devon Books, 1986
Hewins, A. (ed), *The Dillen: Memoirs of a Man of Stratford-upon-Avon*, Elm Tree Books, 1981
Roberts, R., *The Classic Slum*, Penguin, 1971

(d) *Directories, Guide Books and Travel Books*
Anonymous, *Australia as it is*, Charles E. Tuttle, 1967
Tristin, F., *London Journal, 1840*, George Prior, 1980
Knight's *Cyclopaedia of London*, 1851
Murray's *Handbook to Devon & Cornwall*, 1872
Parson & Brailford's *Illustrated Guide To Sheffield and Neighbourhood*, 1862
Schlesinger, M., *Saunterings in and around London*, 1853
Taine, H., *Notes on England*, 1885
White's *Directory of Devon*, 1878-9

Index

Arch, J. 19
Australia 32, 33, 40

begging 9
Belfast 21
Bell, J. 43
Bodmin 38, 39
Booth, C. 9, 15, 24
Botany Bay 32
burglars 14, 15
Burntisland 43

Chadwick, E. 10, 11, 14
Chatham 28, 34
Chartists 20
Clay, J. 30
Collins, W. 42
Conan Doyle, A. 42, 43
corporal punishment 16, 39
cracksmen 15
Criminal Investigation Department 42

Dartmoor Prison 5, 34, 35
Deptford 28
Dickens, C. 6, 16, 33, 37, 43

Edinburgh 43
Engels, F. 6
Eton 25
executions 36, 37, 39

Farnborough 23
"fences" 12, 15
Fenians 20
Fleet Prison 29

garrotting 13
Gilbert, W.G. 24
Gladstone, M. 31
Glasgow 8
Great Massingham 18
Grimstone 17

Hampshire 22
Hawker, J. 19
Hewin, G. 17
Hill, M. 10, 17
Holmes, S. 42, 43
Horsley, J. 7, 8, 9
Hoxton 15
Huddersfield 2
hulks 28
Hume, F. 42
Huntingdon 17

Jefferies, R.
judges 26, 27, 32
Justices of the Peace 6, 25

Kent, C. 40
Kilmarnock 24
Kilvert, F. 18

Lancashire 6, 23
London 11, 16, 20, 21, 22, 24, 26, 27, 29, 30, 36, 42

Manchester 20
Marshalsea Prison 29
Marx, K. 6, 21
Mayhew, H. 13, 14, 16, 21, 32
Mayne, R. 22
Mearns, A. 10
Melbourne 42
Metropolitan Police 3, 7, 22, 23, 42
Middlesex 6
Morrison, A. 36

Napier, C. 20
Newgate Prison 29, 37
New South Wales 33
Newton Stewart 41
Norfolk 17, 18
Norfolk Island 33
Norwich 17
Nottingham 20

oakum 31
Old Bailey 26, 27
Orangemen 21

Pearman, J. 25
Peel, R. 22, 25, 36
Pentonville Prison 28, 29, 31
pickpockets 12, 13, 16
poaching 18, 19
Plymouth 38
Portland Prison 27, 31, 34
Portsmouth 28, 34

Quarterly Review 6, 7, 15

Radnorshire 18
Roberts, R. 25
rookeries 10
Rowan, C. 7
Russell, Lord J. 36

Salford 12, 25
Schlesinger, M. 8, 23, 41
Scotland Yard 23
separate system 30, 31
"Shadow" 8
Sheerness 28, 32
Sheffield 22
silent system 30, 31
Southampton 22
Sydney 32

Taine, H. 26
Tasmania 32
transportation 3, 32, 33
treadwheel 3
Trollope, A. 13

Van Diemen's Land (Tasmania) 32, 33
Vergil 34
Western Australia 32
Whitechapel 13
Woolwich 28
Watson, Dr 42, 43